READING

WEATHER

The Field Guide to Forecasting the Weather

Jim Woodmencey

SECOND EDITION

FALCONGUIDES

GUILFORD, CONNECTICUT
HELENA, MONTANA

AN IMPRINT OF GLOBE PEQUOT PRESS

FALCONGUIDES®

Copyright © 2012 by Morris Book Publishing, LLC
A previous edition was published in 1998 by Falcon Publishing.

FalconGuides is an imprint of Globe Pequot Press.
Falcon, FalconGuides, and Outfit Your Mind are registered trademarks of
Morris Book Publishing, LLC.

Layout: Sue Murray
Project editor: Ellen Urban
Maps: Alena Joy Pearce © Morris Book Publishing, LLC

A previous edition of this book has been cataloged by the Library of
Congress as follows:
Library of Congress Cataloging-in-Publication Data:
Woodmencey, Jim 1957–
  Reading weather : where will you be when the storm hits? / Jim
Woodmencey.
    p.   cm.
  Includes bibliographical references.
  ISBN 1-56044-662-5 (pbk.)
  1. Weather forecasting—Handbooks, manuals, etc. I. Title.
  QC995.48.W66 1998
  551.63—DC21
  98-14715

ISBN 978-0-7627-8236-9

Printed in the United States of America
10 9 8 7 6 5 4 3 2 1

Contents

Acknowledgments

First and foremost, I have to thank Jill Fredston, who edited tirelessly for me every inch of the way. Jill's knowledge of weather and her experience as an author were just the combination of skills I needed.

Second, I must give praise and thanks to meteorologists Knox Williams, Greg Poulos, and Carol Ciliberti for their editing and sage advice.

To the staff of FalconGuides, my gratitude for your help and guidance from start to finish.

The real "fabric" of this book, though, predates all the writing and editing. Some credit is due Professor Bob Yaw, for molding me into a forecaster when he didn't have much to work with. I must also recognize Dr. John Montagne, who taught me that the weather and nature happen outdoors, not in the lab.

This book would also not have come to fruition without the literal mountain of people who have shared weather observations with me from countless outings over the years. These observations helped to disprove many of the theories and forced me to dispense with a number of the thumb-rules I might have had about the weather.

Finally, I cannot possibly thank enough my wife Jan, son Dean, and daughter René for their incredible patience while this book was a work in progress.

Preface

The Nature of the Beast

The snowstorm struck in the middle of the afternoon, with five climbers still well short of the summit. What began with increasing winds and descending clouds quickly turned into a raging snowstorm that lasted for almost three days.

In a fight for their lives, the climbers spent agonizing hours in zero visibility, trying to find their way to safety. For two long, cold nights, they huddled together in an effort to stay warm against temperatures near 20 degrees and a wind-chill factor that made the air feel like it was well below zero.

In the end, the storm won. Three of the five men died. One of the survivors lost toes to frostbite; the other was nearly dead of hypothermia when rescuers finally located him lying helpless in the snow on the side of the mountain.

This happened in early September on the Grand Teton in Wyoming.

These climbers had set out in fine weather. The forecast they'd gotten before leaving for the climb had not mentioned bad weather. They were dressed for a summer climb: tennis shoes or light boots, and a minimum of warm clothing, although some did have waterproof pants and jackets.

They were caught off guard. The weather was not on their schedule. If the storm had held off for another three or four hours, they could have been safely up and well on their way back down the mountain. If the storm had started earlier in the morning, they would have never begun the climb. If the storm had been more "typical" of the season, lasting only a few hours, they could have sat it out and survived. If . . .

If only they had been able to read the weather and make a good decision earlier in the game.

Any outdoor activity can be dangerous when the weather turns foul. A single bolt of lightning on the neighborhood ball field can produce the same result as a blizzard on the summit of Mount Everest. One of the keys to staying safe in the outdoors is the ability to recognize the signs that indicate Mother Nature may be about to ambush you.

The first part of this book (chapters 1–6) will help you understand the basics of meteorology and weather forecasting. The second part of the book (chapters 7–10) will show you weather clues to look for and how to interpret them. Finally, this book will give you some insight into formulating your own forecast, and it will help you make those critical "go" or "no go" decisions that may bring you face-to-face with the beast we call weather.

Unless otherwise noted, weather discussions and Forecast Tips included throughout this book pertain to weather in the Northern Hemisphere—more specifically, to the United States and Canada. However, information in this book applies to weather all over the world. To make a ballpark conversion from the Fahrenheit temperatures given here to Celsius temperatures, subtract 30 and divide by 2.

Weather Basics: Temperature, Pressure, Humidity, and Wind

The Weather

Clear blue skies and a million miles of visibility. Not a breath of wind and the temperature is ideal. The pressure is high and the air is dry.

How can a sky so clear possibly change to leaden gray, fill with electricity, and produce a torrential downpour? How can it become windy enough to knock you down, level your tent, uproot a tree, or tear the roof off your house? How can it become so hot that you pass out from exhaustion, or so cold that the skin on your nose freezes in an instant? How can the air get so moist and the pressure drop so low that a blizzard or a hurricane forms?

You will need to look at least 93 million miles away to find the source for the weather here on Earth. The sun is ultimately responsible for setting our air in motion, and it is the driving force behind every storm.

The Sun and Temperature

The spherical shape of the Earth causes the sun to heat the world unevenly. If you were to shine a flashlight at the globe of the Earth from a distance, you would find that the area around the equator receives the most direct rays of light; hence, the sun heats that area the most. The North and South Poles, on the other hand, receive less direct light, and they do not gain much heat. In fact, for part of the winter the poles receive no sunlight at all.

As you move south from colder air at the North Pole or north from the hot air at the equator, you move into the Temperate Zone. The Temperate Zone extends from 23 degrees to about 66 degrees latitude north and includes most of North America.

The tilt of the Earth on its axis is responsible for the changing seasons, with the most dramatic changes occurring in the more-northern latitudes of the Temperate Zone. From late spring through early fall, the Northern Hemisphere (including the United States) is tilted more toward the sun and receives the greatest and most direct amount of sunlight, which heats the surface and in turn raises daily temperatures. In winter, the Northern Hemisphere tilts away from the direct rays of the sun, and the surface cannot heat up as easily. (See Figures 1A and 1B.)

Temperature Changes with Altitude

Temperature generally decreases as you gain altitude. On average, depending on whether the air is wet or dry, temperature decreases with altitude at a rate of about 3 to 5 degrees F per 1,000 feet of altitude.

A temperature "inversion" occurs when cold air pools at the surface and air temperatures actually increase with altitude (for example, this often happens at night in a valley).

The Land and the Sea

We know there are large-scale differences in the amount of heat received from the sun between the North Pole and the equator. On a slightly smaller scale, the heating of

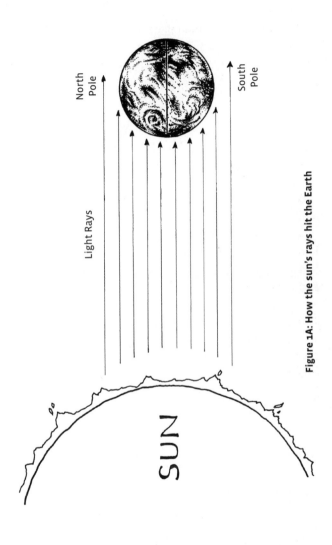

Figure 1A: How the sun's rays hit the Earth

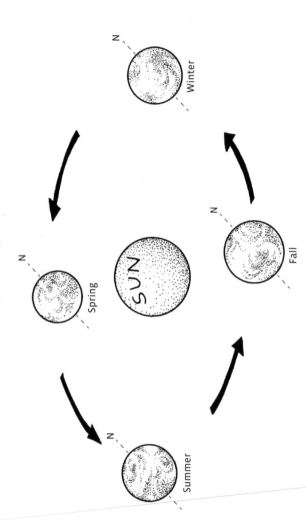

Figure 1B: Seasons in Northern Hemisphere

water also differs significantly from the heating of adjacent land masses, since water does not gain or lose heat as rapidly as land.

We can test this principle with a trip to the beach on a sunny day. During the day, the sun heats the sand more than it heats the water. We can barely walk barefoot in the sand, but the water is refreshingly cool. At night, the sand cools rapidly, while the water temperature remains close to what it was during the hottest part of the day. Globally, then, there is an incredibly complex heating and cooling system in place.

The Atmosphere

The atmosphere—the collection of "air molecules" that surrounds our planet—is about 78 percent nitrogen and 21 percent oxygen. The remaining 1 percent consists of other gases, including water vapor. However, that 1 percent accounts for all the weather we get here on Earth.

The part of the atmosphere that contains our weather extends upward from the surface only about 10 miles, or about 50,000 feet. In comparison to the size of the planet, this layer of atmosphere is relatively thin, about the thickness of the skin on a tomato.

Air has weight. If you could corral those air molecules and weigh them on a scale, you would find that, at sea level, air weighs about 2 pounds per cubic yard. A cubic yard is roughly the storage capacity of a big household refrigerator. However, air is hard to corral, so normally the air is weighed by measuring its "pressure."

Barometric Pressure

"Air pressure" is the amount of force the atmosphere exerts on a surface. Actually, air molecules bouncing around and hitting things create this pressure. Air pressure is commonly measured on a barometer and is referred to as the "barometric pressure." An altimeter, which measures elevation above sea level, is really a barometer in disguise. When barometric pressure decreases, a stationary altimeter will register a gain in altitude because when you climb, the atmosphere grows thinner, exerting less pressure.

Around sea level, air has a pressure of about 15 pounds per square inch. This is also equal to about 30 inches of mercury, or 1,000 millibars. "Inches of mercury" (in. Hg) and "millibars" (mb) are the most common ways of expressing air pressure on a barometer. (See chapter 8 for a more-detailed discussion of barometers and altimeters.)

Pressure Changes with Altitude

The higher you go, the less atmosphere there is above you. That equates to fewer air molecules and lower pressure.

- At 5,000 feet the air pressure is about 15 percent less than it is at sea level.

- At 18,000 feet the pressure is about half of what it is at sea level.

Pressure Changes with Distance

Barometric pressure also changes as you travel horizontally in any direction, assuming you can stay at the same elevation. What makes the pressure change from place to place? Changes in the temperature and the humidity of the air over an area will cause the barometric pressure to fluctuate. Under higher pressure your barometer, if adjusted to a sea-level reading, for instance, would register something above 30.00 in. Hg. Under lower pressure,

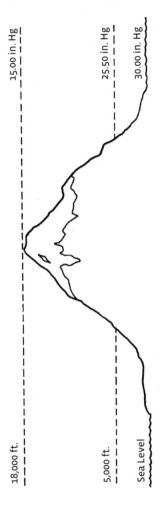

Figure 2: Pressure decreases with altitude

the barometer would read below that. If you were to travel from one area of the country to another and your barometric pressure reading went down, then you would have moved from an area that was under high pressure to an area that is under low pressure (again, assuming no change in elevation). If you stay in one place and your barometric pressure reading goes down, then you can assume that an area of low pressure is moving over you. If the pressure goes up, then high pressure is moving over you. (See chapter 2 for a more-thorough discussion of high and low pressure.)

> ***Forecast Tip!*** When the barometer is changing, so is the weather.

Humidity

"Humidity" is the measure of how much moisture is contained in the air. More correctly, it is the measure of how much water vapor (water as a gas rather than a liquid) the air contains.

"Relative Humidity" (RH) is the relationship between how much moisture is in the air versus how much it is capable of holding. A relative humidity of 50 percent means that the air, at the current temperature, is only halfway to being completely saturated. Above 100 percent humidity, water vapor molecules join together to make liquid drops, or what we see as clouds.

- Warm air can hold more water vapor than cold air.

- Air at 80 degrees F can hold almost four times the water vapor that air at 40 degrees F can hold.

- Air that is saturated (100 percent RH) at 40 degrees F would only have an RH of about 25 percent when warmed to 80 degrees F.

Dew Point

The "dew point temperature" is another way to express humidity. The dew point is the temperature to which the air must be cooled in order to reach saturation (100 percent RH).

- The closer the dew point is to the temperature, the moister the air is.

- High dew points indicate very moist air. Low dew points indicate dry air.

- When the air temperature is warm and the humidity (or dew point) is high—for example, 85 degrees F and 85 percent RH (a dew point of 82 degrees F)—then we say the air is muggy.

- If condensation forms on the outside of your cold beverage on a hot day, then the air was cooled by the beverage container to the dew point. The relative humidity of a thin layer of air adjacent to the surface of your container is 100 percent.

Wind Blows from High to Low Pressure

Temperature and humidity characteristics of the air change from one location to another, and hence, the air pressure will change. When there is a big-enough difference in pressure over a certain distance, then the wind will begin to blow as air moves from high pressure to low pressure.

- The change in pressure over a horizontal distance is a "pressure gradient."

- The bigger the pressure change, the larger the gradient, and the harder the wind will blow.

An example of this is the air in a balloon. When released, the high-pressure air inside the balloon moves out into the room, which contains relatively low-pressure air. The flow is from the balloon to the room, or from high to low. (See chapter 2 for more on how pressure affects weather.)

Forces of the Wind

Wind seldom blows directly from high to low pressure. Forces other than air pressure also influence the wind. Gravity acts on the atmosphere in a downward direction, but it exerts essentially the same force all over the globe. Three other forces, which vary in strength according to the wind speed, will make the final determination about which way the wind blows. These are:

1. **Coriolis effect:** The spin of the Earth on its axis causes the wind that is blowing from high to low pressure to be deflected to the right in the Northern Hemisphere. In the Southern Hemisphere, it causes the wind to turn to the left. This is the Coriolis effect.

2. **Friction:** The roughness of the Earth's surface acts to slow down the wind. The rougher the terrain, the more effect there is from friction.

3. **Centrifugal force:** When you ride a merry-go-round, centrifugal force throws you to the outside of the curved path you are on; and when you drive your

car around a curve, the faster you're moving, the more force there is pulling you toward the outside of the curve. The same thing happens to the wind when it moves in a curved path, causing it to take an outward direction.

The balance of all these forces results in the final wind direction.

Wind Observations

Close to the ground, the wind encounters a lot of friction, which helps counteract the Coriolis effect. Friction slows down the wind. The slower the wind speed, the smaller the Coriolis effect. Therefore, down near ground level, the wind usually blows more in a direct path from high to low pressure.

In the upper atmosphere, there is less friction. As air starts moving from high to low pressure, the Coriolis effect deflects it to the right in the Northern Hemisphere, and to the left in the Southern Hemisphere. The centrifugal force resulting from the Coriolis effect pushes the wind outward regardless of which hemisphere you are in. The result is that the wind blows around high- and low-pressure centers in a curved path.

Use the clouds moving overhead as an indicator of the true wind direction. At ground level the terrain will influence wind direction. Mountains, valleys, canyons, and buildings will change the direction of the wind.

> **Forecast Tip!** If you stand facing the wind in the Northern Hemisphere, low pressure will be off to your right.

1. **Pressure gradient** starts the wind moving from high to low pressure.

2. Near the ground, **friction** slows the wind.

3. In the upper atmosphere, wind is deflected to the right by the **Coriolis effect.**

4. Once air is moving in a curved path, **centrifugal force** pulls it outward.

5. If you stand facing the wind, **low pressure** will be to your right.

The Jet Stream

Think of the jet stream as a river of wind flowing at an altitude around 30,000 feet, unaffected by surface friction. Jet streams, as with all winds, are caused by differences in air temperature and pressure. The jet stream is generally defined as the area of the strongest winds in the atmosphere and it correspondingly follows a path that draws a line between the coldest and warmest air in the atmosphere. The strength of the jet stream will vary depending on how big these differences are in temperature and pressure. The bigger the difference, the stronger the jet stream.

- Jet stream winds are typically around 100 miles per hour.

- The jet stream can be several hundred miles wide and several thousand feet thick.

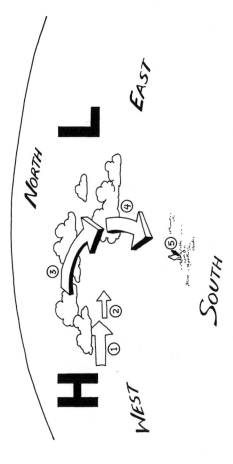

Figure 3: Wind flow from high to low

- In the winter, the main jet stream over North America migrates farther south as colder air moves south.

- In the summer, the jet stream migrates back to the north.

- Several different jet streams can exist in the atmosphere at the same time.

Highs, Lows, Fronts, and Storms

2

As the world turns, so does the atmosphere above. Since the atmosphere is not fixed to the globe, it can move faster, lag behind, or even move in a direction opposite to that of the Earth's rotation.

The atmosphere is also moving up and down like a seesaw, with warm air rising and cold air sinking. As all the forces in the atmosphere struggle to reach a happy medium, pressure systems develop.

High Pressure

If a region of high pressure is dominant in the upper levels of the atmosphere, then air will begin to move away, or "diverge," from its center and seek lower pressure.

As air diverges from a high-pressure center, the Coriolis effect turns it to the right. A clockwise circulation will develop around the center of a high. On the weather map, high-pressure centers are marked with an "H."

> *Forecast Tip!* Under an area of "high" pressure, the air is sinking, which means it is warming and drying out, and is unable to condense water vapor. Therefore, clouds and precipitation cannot form. Good weather generally prevails.

Low Pressure

Eventually, air that is moving from a region of high pressure will run into an area of more-dominant low pressure.

As air moves into a region of low pressure, it will begin "converging" toward the center. This forces air upward. Upward motion is needed to build clouds.

As air converges toward a low-pressure center, the Coriolis effect will turn it to the right. A counterclockwise circulation will develop around the center of a low. On the weather map, low-pressure centers are marked with an "L."

Forecast Tip! Within an area of low pressure, the air is rising. When air rises, it generally cools. Eventually, it may condense water vapor, causing cloud formation and perhaps precipitation. Bad weather generally prevails.

For H:
High-Pressure Center
Clockwise Circulation
Diverging Flow

For L:
Low-Pressure Center
Counterclockwise Circulation
Converging Flow

Figure 4: Circulation around highs and lows

Waves and Pressure Systems

As high- and low-pressure systems develop around the globe, they link together into waves, alternating between "ridges" of high pressure and "troughs" of low pressure. Waves are generally seen best on a map of the jet stream. (For good places to find quality weather maps, see chapter 3.)

On the weather map, "isobars" are lines of constant pressure. They work just like elevation contours on a topographical map. Read a weather map with isobars on it just as you would a topographical map. Areas of high pressure make hills, while areas of low pressure appear as valleys.

Forecast Tip! The more tightly packed the isobars are, the steeper the pressure gradient and the stronger the winds, much like a cliff on a topographical map.

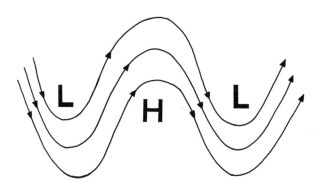

Figure 5: Waves with pressure gradient

A Mass of Air

Within these areas of high and low pressure, the air will have its own character depending on whether it is originating near the poles or the equator, as well as over land or water. An "air mass" is a large volume of air in which the moisture (humidity) and temperature characteristics are similar over a large geographical area. Air masses are grouped by their geographic origins:

- Continental air originates over land and is dry.

- Maritime air originates over an ocean and is wet.

- Polar air originates near the poles and is colder than the air it is moving over.

- Tropical air originates near the equator and is warmer than the air it is moving over.

When you combine "wet or dry" with "cold or warm," there are four basic air mass types (see Table 1). When studying the weather, it is helpful to know the characteristics of the various types of air masses.

Continental-Polar, Maritime-Tropical, and Maritime-Polar are the most common types of air masses in the United States. Continental-Tropical air mass is less common, and is found over large desert areas.

Continental-Polar air masses move south in the winter— for example, from northern Canada. When they move over warmer land or water, they produce snow. This is especially true over the Great Lakes or along the eastern slopes of the Rockies.

Maritime-Tropical air masses moving north out of the Gulf of Mexico can cause a variety of severe weather, including heavy rains or thunderstorms over the central, southern, and eastern parts of the United States. This is especially true when a Maritime-Tropical air mass collides with a Continental-Polar air mass. Maritime-Polar air masses commonly come out of the Pacific in the winter months, bringing rain and snow to the western half of the United States.

Table 1: Air Mass Type	
Continental-Polar	Dry and Cold
Continental-Tropical	Dry and Warm
Maritime-Polar	Wet and Cold
Maritime-Tropical	Wet and Warm

From Air Mass to Front to Storm

The boundary between two air masses is called a "front." Across a front there will be a contrast in temperature and moisture (humidity) characteristics.

If there is a sharp contrast across a front—for example, with very cold air pushing against very warm air—then some wave motion or spin will start to develop. As this spin begins to turn in a counterclockwise direction, low pressure will form at the apex, and a storm is born.

Types of Fronts

Several types of fronts can form in a developing storm system. Refer to Figure 6A to see how fronts appear on a weather map. The "vertical profile" will help you visualize how they look as they extend up through the atmosphere (see Figure 6B).

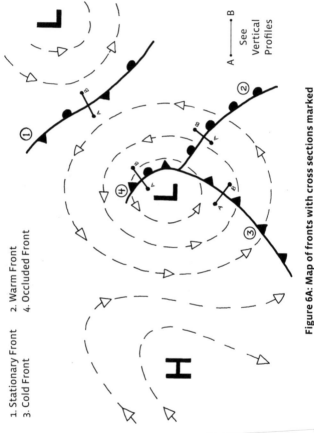

1. Stationary Front   2. Warm Front
3. Cold Front   4. Occluded Front

A •———• B
See
Vertical
Profiles

Figure 6A: Map of fronts with cross sections marked

Figure 6B: Vertical profiles of fronts

warm

cold

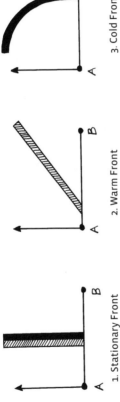

1. Stationary Front

2. Warm Front

3. Cold Front

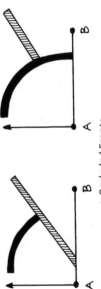

4. Occluded Fronts

Troughs

A "trough" of low pressure may exist by itself in the upper levels of the atmosphere. A trough is like a "valley" of low pressure moving in the flow aloft. The clouds and precipitation associated with a trough may mimic a cold front. Troughs appear on some weather maps as a dashed line.

Similar to a trough is an "upper-level disturbance" or "shortwave." This is an area of low pressure circulating higher in the atmosphere, but with no identifiable fronts associated with it at the surface.

Life Cycle of a Storm System

A storm system goes through its own evolution from birth to death. It will gain strength and energy as it starts to spin into a counterclockwise rotation. Fronts will form, dispense their energy, and then dissolve. Eventually, the storm will disintegrate and become a simple air mass (see Figure 7).

Table 2: Stationary Front	
Definition	Boundary between warm and cold air that is not moving much. May develop into warm or cold front.
Clouds	Form in the vicinity of the front, but sometimes very few clouds exist.
Precipitation	Usually found very near the front, but sometimes none is produced.
Vertical Profile	Stands straight up and down, separates warm air from cold air.
On the Weather Map	Appears as alternating red and blue line, with half-circles and triangles pointing on opposite sides of the line (see Figure 6A).

Table 3: Warm Front	
Definition	Boundary between warmer air that is riding over the top of cooler air.
Clouds	Can precede front by several hundred miles.
Precipitation	Can occur along and ahead of the front.
Vertical Profile	Slopes gradually upward from the ground as it rides over cooler air.
On the Weather Map	Appears as a red line, with half-circles on one side of the line pointing in the direction the front is moving (see Figure 6A).

Table 4: Cold Front	
Definition	Boundary between colder air that is pushing up warmer air ahead of it.
Clouds	Found along and just ahead of the front.
Precipitation	Occurs along and just ahead of the front.
Vertical Profile	Slopes steeply upward from the ground away from warmer air.
On the Weather Map	Appears as a blue line, with triangles on one side pointing in the direction the front is moving (see Figure 6A).

Table 5: Occluded Front	
Definition	When a cold front catches up to a warm front, an occluded front forms.
Clouds	Can mimic a warm or cold front.
Precipitation	Can mimic a warm or cold front.
Vertical Profile	Cold front either rides over the top or pushes underneath a warm front.
On the Weather Map	Appears as a purple line, with alternating half-circles and triangles on one side pointing in the direction the front is moving (see Figure 6A).

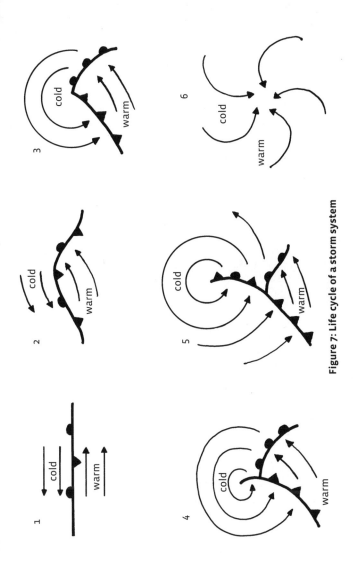

Figure 7: Life cycle of a storm system

Spinning Storms and Rugged Terrain

Storms act very much like spinning tops. When you release a spinning top on a smooth, level surface (like a glass table), it will spin energetically for a long time.

When you let the same top go on a rough surface (like pebbled concrete), it starts to wobble and slows immediately. Most storms will act the same way when they move inland off the ocean. Ever notice how hurricanes slow after they make landfall?

Storms that move over mountain ranges can also be disrupted; they often split apart or are redirected by the mountainous topography.

> **Forecast Tip!** Only the largest and strongest of storms can move across mountainous terrain unimpeded, without disruption.

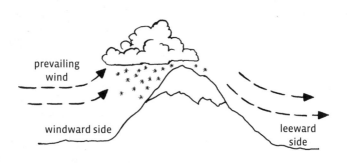

Figure 8: Cloud lifting in the mountains

Mountains Can Help, Too

Instead of being disruptive, mountains sometimes assist the lifting motion of storms and fronts. On the windward side of a mountain (the side facing into the prevailing wind), where air is forced upward and cooled to its dew point quite readily, precipitation can be heavier. On the leeward side of a mountain (the side that faces away from the prevailing wind), air tends to sink and dry out, with less precipitation.

Understanding Weather Forecasts

3

When planning any outdoor activity, whether it is a picnic or a mountaineering expedition, it is most important to arm yourself with as much information about the weather as possible before you leave.

You must also understand what the forecast says, so that there are few surprises once you are outdoors and subject to the weather.

Find a Source

A wide assortment of weather sources and information is available. The majority of the graphics and text information you will find started out as raw data from the National Weather Service. That data is then redistributed through a variety of outlets, with varying levels of interpretation. The following is a list of places where you can usually find a local forecast and a basic weather map showing the position of fronts, highs, lows, and temperatures. For the latest maps and best selection of forecast products, you can't beat the Internet.

Newspapers: There is a good chance that the weather forecast you read in the daily newspaper was prepared many hours before the paper hit your doorstep, so it may be of limited value.

Television: Find a station with a real meteorologist who formulates his or her own local forecast. Local stations focus on local weather. The Weather Channel provides a good overall national view, as well as local zone forecast information from the National Weather Service (NWS).

The Internet: There is almost too much weather information available these days on the World Wide Web. Most weather forecasts you find are using NWS information and reformatting it. Therefore, a good starting place might be the website for the NWS office closest to you. Here you can find both local and national forecasts, maps, and other weather products. A few other good sources for weather maps and forecasts are: www.weather.com, www.intellicast.com, and wxweb.meteostar.com.

Private Weather Services: More complete and reliable weather data, along with custom forecasts, can be obtained from a number of weather consulting firms and private meteorologists. One example would be the author's website, www.mountainweather.com.

Forecast Tip! Always check the date and the time on any weather forecast, text, or graphic, to be sure you are looking at the most recent data.

Forecast Tip! Always check the location for which the forecast is issued to be sure that it is the closest one available for your destination.

Start by Understanding Why

Begin your preplanning by reading or listening to a "discussion" or "synopsis" of the current weather situation. A weather discussion explains how storm systems, highs, lows, fronts, and so forth are expected to act over the next few days. Each National Weather Service office issues its own discussion with specific information for the state or surrounding forecast area.

Find these at individual NWS office websites under "Forecast Discussion." Be aware that the wording is often abbreviated, so reading these takes some getting used to. The forecast discussion explains the general weather pattern and what is causing the weather, which can make the local weather forecast much more meaningful.

Basic Forecast Parts

Most forecasts will include cloud cover, precipitation, temperature, and wind information. Clouds and precipitation are presented with a variety of descriptive terms and require some interpretation. Temperature and wind are usually given with a specific number range, and are self-explanatory.

Most people would agree that the precipitation portion of the forecast is the part they pay attention to the most.

> **Forecast Tip!** Most people interpret any mention of rain or snow in the forecast to mean that it will rain or snow, which is not always the case. Listen for any terms expressing uncertainty within the forecast, and try not to discount any probability that might be included.

Less-Certain Forecasts

In essence, weather forecasts are expressions of uncertainty. The wording is a direct reflection of the forecaster's confidence in the upcoming weather. Forecasts can contain any variety of terms used to describe the probability of upcoming weather. Wording like "possibly" or "chance of" should indicate that something might or might not occur.

When the weather is "unsettled," the pattern may be very complex, making it difficult to forecast clouds and precipitation exactly. This may also be due to the timing of arriving or departing weather systems. On these days, there is less confidence, and hence less certainty in the forecast.

An example of a forecast that is less certain: "Partly to mostly cloudy skies with a chance of showers or thunderstorms."

More-Certain Forecasts

When the weather is more "settled," the pattern is more consistent and will bring either persistently good or bad weather. In this case, the forecast will be more certain. This is usually the case when weather systems are not moving much.

Examples of forecasts that are more certain: "Cloudy skies with rain showers and thunderstorms." "Mostly sunny skies today. Clear skies tonight. Sunny skies tomorrow."

What Is "Partly Cloudy"?

Forecasts of sky conditions are usually the first part of a weather forecast. Here are the most commonly used terms and their meanings:

- Clear is used in place of the word sunny at night.

- Partly sunny is technically the same as partly cloudy, but is often perceived as something between partly and mostly cloudy.

- Fair is a generic term, used to indicate generally good weather. There may be some high clouds around, but usually less than 40 percent coverage.

Table 6: Sky Conditions and Cloud Coverage	
Sky Conditions	*Cloud Coverage*
Cloudy	90 to 100 percent
Mostly Cloudy	70 to 80 percent
Partly Cloudy	30 to 60 percent
Mostly Sunny	10 to 30 percent
Sunny	10 percent or less

What Is "Chance of Showers"?

"Probability of precipitation" is used to describe the likelihood of occurrence of a measurable amount of precipitation at any given point within the forecast area. Measurable is defined as at least 0.01 inches (0.2 mm) of water equivalent (from rain or melted snow). That is enough rain to completely wet a road or trail, and enough snow to evenly cover the ground.

- "A 30 percent chance of rain" should also mean that there is a 70 percent chance it won't rain.

- If the forecast just says "rain" or "thunderstorms," then the chances of occurrence are thought to be better than about 75 percent.

Table 7: Probability of Precipitation	
Probability Value	"Uncertain" Term
10 to 20 percent	Slight Chance
30 to 50 percent	Chance
60 to 70 percent	Likely
80 to 100 percent	(usually no term used; certainty is high)

Precipitation Types Defined

Table 8: Precipitation Types: Summer	
Shower	Intermittent or a brief period of rainfall.
Rain	Steady precipitation that lasts for several hours.
Thundershower	Implies a rain shower, with at least cloud-to-cloud lightning. Potential for 1 to 2 bolts to strike the ground.
Thunderstorm	Implies brief (often heavy) rain and/or gusty winds and some lightning strikes. Can last 10 minutes to several hours.
Strong T-storm	Implies heavy rainfall and/or small hail and/or gusty winds up to about 60 mph. Potential for many lightning strikes.
Severe T-storm	Implies heavy downpours and/or large hail, and/or winds greater than about 60 mph, and/or tornadoes. Potential for numerous lightning strikes.

Table 9: Precipitation Types: Winter	
Snow Flurry	Light snowfall that usually does not produce measurable accumulation.
Snow Shower	Snow that starts and stops and usually produces measurable accumulation.
Snow	Steady snowfall that lasts for several hours, with accumulation.
Freezing Rain	Rain that hits a cold surface or object of 32 degrees F (0 degrees C) or less and freezes on impact.
Sleet	Solid grains of ice that form when raindrops hit colder air as they fall from the clouds. Sleet can also form from the partial melting and refreezing of falling snowflakes.

Wind

When wind speed is not assigned a number value in the forecast, it may appear as a descriptive term. *Note: The criteria may vary for different parts of the country.*

- "High wind warnings" are usually issued for sustained winds of over 40 mph that are expected to last for one hour, or longer. This warning is also used if wind gusts are expected to exceed about 60 mph.

Forecast Tip! You can often estimate the wind speed up at ridgetop level in the mountains by doubling the wind speed in the valley.

Table 10: Description of Wind and Sustained Wind Speed	
Description of Wind	**Sustained Wind Speed**
Breezy, Brisk, or Blustery	15 to 25 mph
Windy or Very Windy	25 to 40 mph
High Winds	Over 40 mph

Next Step: Study the Maps

Surface maps plotted with highs, lows, and fronts provide a picture of where various weather features are located. See chapter 10 for examples and discussion. You can also find maps in the newspaper, on television, or on the Internet. Familiarize yourself with these features and their meanings. (Refer back to chapter 2 for a review.)

See the Picture and Watch the Movie

Weather maps on television and the Internet offer additional features.

- Satellite photos show the current cloud cover, but not necessarily if there is precipitation.

- Radar images show where precipitation might be currently falling. The color-coded scale will indicate how heavy that precipitation may be.

- A "loop" is a movie comprised of hourly satellite photos or radar maps created over the previous twelve hours or so. The loop gives an idea of the movement of clouds or precipitation, and how fast they may be approaching your location. A loop is a much more valuable forecasting tool than a single frame.

Forecaster's Preplanning Checklist

- ❏ Get a good briefing of the general weather situation from a National Weather Service discussion or the Weather Channel.

- ❏ Get the local zone forecast and extended outlook. See how they change from day to day, and note how accurate they have been.

- ❏ Study the current surface weather map and its features.

- ❏ Study the projected weather maps and features.

- ❏ Study satellite photos and loops; check the radar, too.

- ❏ Know which storm systems are coming or going.

- ❏ Be prepared for the extremes or changes in the forecasted temperatures, winds, or precipitation. Adjust your plans accordingly.

Summer
Weather Problems

4

Summer is the season when we expect the most pleasant weather of the year, and it is also when we spend the most time outdoors. The summer season also brings some of nature's most unpredictable and violent weather. We will consider "summer weather" to be the type of weather you would expect from spring through fall (roughly from April to November) in the Northern Hemisphere.

Summer Hazards

On average in the United States, about 55 people a year are killed by lightning, another 55 people are killed by tornadoes, and about 100 people die in floods annually. Severe thunderstorms, tornadoes, torrential downpours, and hurricanes present a threat to those who spend a lot of time outdoors because they can often occur with little warning. Understanding and recognizing the early-warning signs of severe weather may save your life.

An Unstable Atmosphere

Thunderstorms are caused by "convection"—the action you get when you heat a pan of water on the stove. With enough heat, the water boils. Similarly, when the atmosphere is heated from the ground up, the moisture in the air will begin to "boil" and form thunderstorms.

There must be moisture and "instability" in the atmosphere in order for thunderstorms to form. "Instability" is a measure of the rate at which air temperature changes with increasing altitude. Generally, air cools at the rate of about 4 degrees F per 1,000 feet of elevation gain (6.5 degrees C per 1,000 meters). In a thunderstorm situation, air cools at a rate much greater than this.

- Air is considered unstable if it is rising and continues to rise.

- The faster the air temperature decreases with height, the more unstable the air. Instability is created by increased heating of the ground by the sun, or by cooler air moving above relatively warm air.

- Air is considered stable if it is not rising.

- If air temperature increases with height, then the air is stable.

Faster rates of cooling with increasing altitude and greater instability can be caused by more solar heating at the surface, or by an influx of warmer air in the lower levels of the atmosphere, brought about, for example, by a southerly wind flow. Alternatively, the same thing can happen when an area of colder air in the upper levels of the atmosphere moves over warmer air at the surface, which can happen when an upper-level trough passes through.

Air will continue to rise as long as it is warmer than the air it is rising through. As air rises, cools, and condenses, clouds form and precipitation can occur. With thunderstorms, air is rising and condensing rapidly with a lot of energy being generated. Eventually, that energy has to be released.

Table 11: Stability Chart	
If ...	Then ...
Temperature is cold aloft and warm near the ground	Air is unstable
Temperature is warm aloft and cold near the ground	Air is stable
Temperature is warm aloft and warm near the ground	Air is stable
Temperature is cold aloft and cold near the ground	Conditionally unstable *
*Air is stable until ground is heated; then it can become unstable.	

Thunderstorm Facts

The more unstable the atmosphere is, the bigger the thunderstorms will be. "Thunderstorms" imply that there will be thunder. There cannot be thunder without lightning.

Prime time for thunderstorm development is during the heat of the day, in the afternoon and evening hours. However, thunderstorms are possible at any time of the day or night. Nocturnal (nighttime) thunderstorms are usually the result of a front or upper-level disturbance that is moving through an area.

Mountains provide extra lift to developing thunderstorms, especially when the wind flow is at 90 degrees (perpendicular) to the orientation of the mountain range. Thunderstorms occur about five times more frequently over mountains and large plateaus than they do over flat terrain or coastal regions. However, the biggest and most dangerous thunderstorms—"supercell" storms—usually form over relatively flat, open terrain because they can continue to spread out and develop without being disrupted by rough terrain. Supercells develop most often in the Great Plains states, and can spawn tornadoes.

- The larger the thunderstorm, the heavier and more widespread the rainfall can be.

- One 15-minute thunderstorm can dump 100 million gallons of water.

- The taller the thunderstorm (the higher the clouds extend vertically into the atmosphere), the greater the likelihood of hail or severe weather.

- Lightning usually precedes heavy rainfall in a thunderstorm.

- Generally speaking, the more lightning strikes a thunderstorm produces, the heavier the rainfall will be.

Forecast Tip! The earlier in the day clouds start building, the earlier in the afternoon thunderstorms can occur.

Cloudbursts and Microbursts

In a very unstable atmosphere, stronger thunderstorms can produce brief periods of very dangerous weather. Tremendous damage can be caused by heavy rains, wind gusts, or hail.

Cloudbursts are heavy sheets of rain that fall suddenly over a small area as the result of a very moist, unstable atmosphere. They may produce more than 4 inches of rain in less than 1 hour.

Microbursts are strong downdrafts of wind that come out of a thunderstorm. Usually, microbursts will occur out ahead of a developing line of thunderstorms, reaching speeds of 50 to 150 mph. Microbursts affect an area less than 3 miles long and last for about 10 minutes. They can be wet or dry.

Hailstorms

Hail forms inside a thunderstorm that has very strong updrafts and downdrafts. Water droplets move up and down within a cloud, passing through the "freezing level" (where the temperature is 32 degrees F) several times; each time they are coated with successive layers of ice. Updrafts must be strong enough to support the weight of the forming hailstones. Stronger updrafts can form larger hail.

- The updraft speed required to support 0.75-inch-diameter hail is 37 mph. To support baseball-sized hail, updraft speeds must be about 100 mph.

- Baseball-sized hail also falls out of the cloud at a speed of about 100 mph, which would be like getting hit with a major league fastball!

- Hail falls out of only a small part of the whole thunderstorm, typically falling in a swath that measures 0.5 to 1 mile wide and 5 to 10 miles long.

- More hail falls in the mountains than in valleys because it often melts before it reaches the lower elevations, where the atmosphere is warmer.

Forecast Tip! The darker the base of the thunderstorm, the more likely it is to produce hail, a heavy downpour, or gusty winds.

Lightning Facts

In the United States, about 100 people are killed by lightning every year; many times that number are injured. Alaska is the only state that has not reported a lightning-related death or injury. Florida has the highest number of lightning fatalities per year. Lightning deaths have occurred in every month of the year, with July and August having the highest incidence.

- Only about 30 percent of the people struck by lightning each year are killed, which means that there is about a 70 percent chance of surviving a direct hit.

- About 80 percent of all lightning discharges remain inside clouds and never strike the ground.

- Heat lightning is simply lightning that is on the horizon, too far away for the thunder to be heard.

- Thunder can be heard when the storm is about 15 to 20 miles away if there are no obstructions, such as mountains.

Forecast Tip! Lightning can strike up to 5 miles away from the base of a thunderstorm. You don't need to be under it to be hit.

Forecast Tip! The most dangerous time for a fatal strike is before the storm is directly overhead.

Timing Lightning to Thunder

Lightning travels at the speed of light. Thunder travels at the speed of sound, which is slower than the speed of light. Therefore, lightning is seen before the thunder is heard.

You can time how far away the lightning is by counting in seconds (one-thousand-one, one-thousand-two, etc.) from the time you see the flash to the time you hear the thunder. Take the number of seconds and divide by 5 to get the distance in miles.

Lightning Safety

The chances of being hit by lightning increase if you spend a lot of time outdoors. Mountain climbers, hikers, cowboys, farmers, golfers, fishermen, and ballplayers are especially prone to being struck by lightning. Swimming or boating during thunderstorms is also dangerous, as lightning does strike water.

- When a thunderstorm is approaching, get off the water, get off the ridgetops, and get out of that field!

- Retreat to your house or car, lie down in a dry ditch, or try to lie as low as possible.

- On an exposed ridge, sit on an insulated pad or backpack. Be sure you are not in a natural watercourse, like a gully; these will conduct ground currents when bolts hit.

- Get away from metal objects, including fences, metal climbing hardware, golf clubs, aluminum rod cases, aluminum walking poles, backpacking cook gear, etc.

- Never stand under a lone tree. Being in a grove of trees of similar height is a better option.

- If you are in a bad position and out of options, keep moving. This is only a theory, but lightning seems to have a harder time connecting with a moving object.

Summer Weather Watches and Warnings

In spring and summer, the National Weather Service will issue "watches" and "warnings" for a variety of severe weather, including severe thunderstorms, tornadoes, and flash floods. Forecast conditions must meet certain criteria.

Table 12: Summer Weather Watches and Warnings	
Severe Thunderstorm Watch	Conditions are favorable for the development of severe thunderstorms. Watch may be in effect for several hours.
Severe Hail Thunderstorm Warning	Issued when a thunderstorm produces hail of 0.75 of an inch or larger and/or wind is greater than about 60 mph.
Tornado Watch	Conditions are favorable for the development of tornadoes.
Tornado Warning	Issued when a tornado is indicated by radar or by a storm spotter (visual observation).
Flash Flood Watch	Indicates that flash flooding of rivers or small streams is a possibility.
Flash Flood Warning	Issued when rapid flooding of rivers and streams is imminent or already occurring.

Forecast Tip! By the time a severe-weather warning is issued, it may be too late to escape nature's wrath. So, when a watch is issued, you should carefully consider your course of action. This is the time to seek shelter or safety.

Winter
Weather Problems

5

Winter offers great opportunities for outdoor recreation—skiing, mountaineering, snowshoeing, hunting, ice-fishing, and snowmobiling, to name a few. We will consider "winter weather" to be the type of weather you would expect from fall through spring, or from roughly November to April in the Northern Hemisphere.

Winterlike weather conditions with below-freezing temperatures and snowfall are also possible in the summer months in Alaska, and in the mountains of the western United States and Canada. Even parts of New England, like Mount Washington, can experience winter weather in midsummer.

Winter Hazards

Winter conditions can be very dangerous and potentially fatal. Hypothermia and frostbite are the major concerns if you are not properly clothed and equipped. Hypothermia is a lowering of the body's core temperature, which results from exposure to cold temperatures or cool, wet weather. Frostbite is the freezing of exposed flesh at temperatures well below the freezing point (see Table 13 on page 50).

Cold temperatures alone are not the biggest problem. Winds in combination with cold air can create a dangerous "wind chill." Wind in combination with snow can lead to blizzard conditions, reducing visibility to near zero and turning simple travel into a nightmare. There really is no such thing as a "typical" storm. Each one has unique characteristics. While there is some consistency as to where winter storms tend to form, determining the path they will take is what presents the greatest forecast challenge.

Table 13: Wind-Chill Chart																	
Air Temperature (°F)																	
Calm	40	35	30	25	20	15	10	5	0	-5	-10	-15	-20	-25	-30	-35	-40
5	36	31	25	19	13	7	1	-5	-11	-16	-22	-28	-34	-40	-46	-52	-57
10	34	27	21	15	9	3	-4	-10	-16	-22	-28	-35	-41	-47	-53	-59	-66
15	32	25	19	13	6	0	-7	-13	-19	-26	-32	-39	-45	-51	-58	-64	-71
20	30	24	17	11	4	-2	-9	-15	-22	-29	-35	-42	-48	-55	-61	-68	-74
25	29	23	16	9	3	-4	-11	-17	-24	-31	-37	-44	-51	-58	-64	-71	-78
30	28	22	15	8	1	-5	-12	-19	-26	-33	-39	-46	-53	-60	-67	-73	-80
35	28	21	14	7	0	-7	-14	-21	-27	-34	-41	-48	-55	-62	-69	-76	-82
40	27	20	13	6	-1	-8	-15	-22	-29	-36	-43	-50	-57	-64	-71	-78	-84
45	26	19	12	5	-2	-9	-16	-23	-30	-37	-44	-51	-58	-65	-72	-79	-86

Wind Speed (mph)

Frostbite occurs in 15 minutes or less with wind-chill temperatures less than minus 20° F.

Wind speeds greater than 45 mph have little additional effect.

Big Snowstorm Formula

There are several factors that can lead to a heavy snowfall–producing storm, but all those factors occurring together at once is not that common.

- There must be below-freezing air involved at all elevations.

- Colder air aloft coming from a northerly direction (NW to NE) will help to keep the atmosphere unstable.

- Warmer air at lower levels coming from a southerly direction (SW to SE) can bring more moisture, but the air still must be near freezing.

- A strong jet stream located directly overhead or just south of your location is ideal.

> **Forecast Tip!** Big snowstorms that last for many hours (or even days) will be associated with a large and often slow-moving low-pressure system.

> **Forecast Tip!** Smaller snowstorms will be related to a faster-moving front, trough, an upper-level disturbance, or some other localized effect.

Winter Storm Origins

Pacific Storms: The Gulf of Alaska is a breeding ground for low-pressure systems. These may begin by affecting south-central and southeast Alaska before dropping south along the West Coast of North America. From there, they may track inland anywhere from British Columbia to southern California, depending on where the jet stream is steering them. From the West Coast, they will move eastward over the Rockies. The size of the storm, its track, and how well it maintains its energy will determine where the greatest precipitation will fall.

Some of these Pacific storms will end up tracking all the way to the Atlantic Ocean, never really losing much of their energy. This will occur in times of a strong "zonal" flow, when the jet stream is running west to east across the entire United States. In this case, the jet stream is usually strong, and storms will advance at a pace of about 500 miles per day.

Pineapple Express: Some Gulf of Alaska storms will also involve a long stream of tropical moisture feeding into the storm from farther south in the Pacific, near Hawaii. This is the "pineapple" part of the storm. In this case, a very wet, west-to-southwesterly flow can hammer the western United States for many days.

Upslope Snowstorms: "Upslope" storms occur when the center of a low-pressure system is positioned to the east of the Continental Divide. The circulation around the low-pressure center causes a wind flow from an east-to-northeast direction, or "up the slope." The rising terrain from the Plains States toward the east slope of the Rocky Mountains acts to "lift" the air. This additional upward motion enhances the condensation and cloud-formation process, which can lead to heavy snowfall. To a lesser extent, upslope storms can occur along the east side of the Appalachian Mountains.

Alberta Clippers: These storms form east of the Continental Divide in Canada and then move south and east across the northern tier of the United States. These "clippers" from Alberta are usually small and fast-moving snowstorms.

Nor'easters: These low-pressure systems form along the East Coast of the United States and move north toward New England. The circulation around these lows causes a northeasterly flow into the East Coast. Sometimes these storms develop very quickly, combining with an upper-level disturbance coming out of the central part of the country, and they go off like a bomb. Blizzard conditions can develop in less than 12 hours, with winds of 70 mph or higher.

Cape Hatteras Lows: As cold water in the Atlantic moves south in the Labrador Current, it meets warmer water flowing north from the Gulf Stream current. Where these two currents meet, just off the North Carolina coast, is a breeding ground for storm systems that affect the Mid-Atlantic States.

Figure 9: Winter storm origins

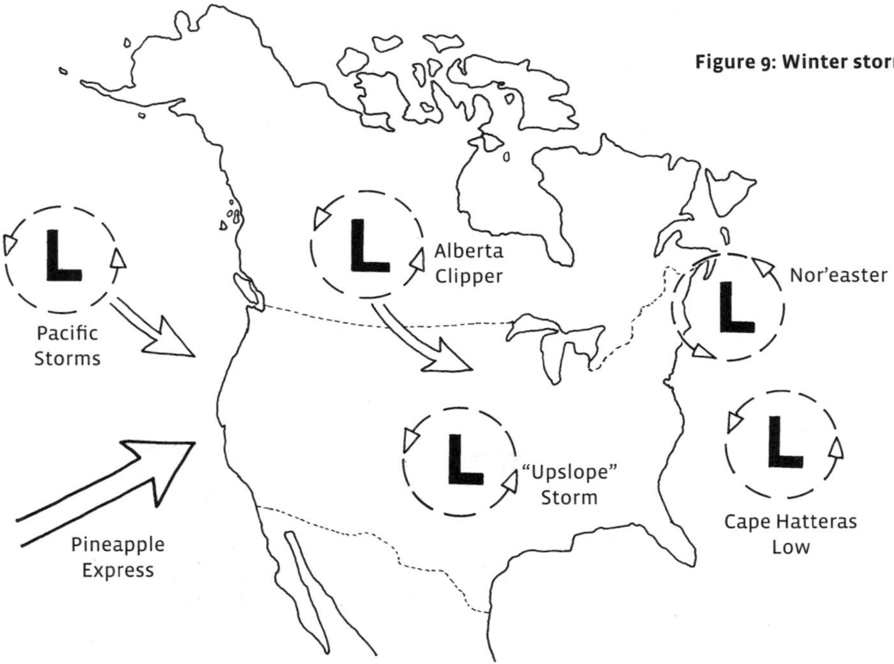

Snow without a Storm

Lake-Effect Snow: Do you have a big lake nearby? "Lake-effect" snowstorms occur when the wind moves colder air from a northerly direction over relatively warm water. This creates localized instability, and with a great moisture source already in place, the result can be heavy snowfall downwind of the lake.

Warm Air Overrunning: When a cold polar air mass is in place at the surface and a warmer tropical air mass moves up from the south, the warmer air will "overrun" the cold air. The warmer air is then lifted upward, forming clouds that are capable of producing snow. No storm system is present, but steady snow can fall for many hours or days in this situation, which is common in the central United States.

Mountain-Effect Snow: The mountains are capable of taking the most benign-looking weather system and turning it into a big dumping of snow. This is due to "orographic lifting," or the added lift that mountains give the air. More lift yields more precipitation, and the larger the mountain, the greater the lifting effect. Lifting is optimized when the flow aloft is perpendicular to the mountain range. For the western United States west of the Continental Divide, a west to northwesterly wind flow, along with a little moisture at mountain elevation, is all that is needed for orographic snowfall. *Note: This is similar to the "upslope" effect that occurs with snowstorms east of the Continental Divide, but orographic snowfall described here is on a more-localized scale.*

Local Convergence Zones: The local topography can also wring out copious amounts of snow when there is little, if any, weather occurring nearby. Canyons and mountain passes act to compress or "converge" the air as it flows through them. Much like water flowing into a narrow section of river, air will tend to stack up when it flows into narrowing terrain. This converging flow causes the air flowing in to be lifted, which in turn will cause more of the available moisture in the atmosphere to condense and precipitate out, producing localized snowfall. Many areas of the United States have their own known "convergence zones." This type of convergence occurs during storms as well, and localized heavy snowfall usually results.

Table 14: Winter Weather Advisories	
Winter Weather Advisory	Issued when a mixture of precipitation is expected, such as snow, sleet, and freezing rain or freezing drizzle.
Snow Advisory	Issued when snowfall is expected to be between 2 and 6 inches in 12 hours. Some mountain locations have snow advisories issued for 4- to 7-inch accumulations in 12 hours.
Blowing Snow Advisory	Issued when wind-driven snow intermittently reduces visibility to 0.25 mile or less. Travel may be hampered. Strong winds create blowing snow by picking up old or new snow.
Freezing Rain Advisory	Generally used when the intensity of freezing rain is light, with accumulations of less than 0.25 inch.
Sleet Advisory	Used when sleet accumulations of less than 0.25 inch are expected.

Table 15: Winter Weather Warnings	
Heavy Snow Warning	Used when snowfall is expected to exceed 6 inches in 12 hours, or 8 inches or more in 24 hours. (Some mountain locations use 8 inches or more in 12 hours, or 10 inches or more in 24 hours).
Winter Storm Warning	Issued when heavy snow and some wind are imminent or very likely. This may be in combination with sleet or freezing rain.
Blizzard Warning	Issued when strong winds of 35 mph or greater, cold temperatures, and considerable falling and/or blowing snow frequently drop visibility to 0.25 mile or less. These conditions are expected to last for 3 hours or longer.
Ice Storm Warning	Issued when ice accumulations during a freezing rain event are expected to be 0.25 inch or greater.
Sleet Warning	Issued when sleet is expected to accumulate to 0.5 inch or more. (This is rare.)

Advisories

The National Weather Service will issue occasional winter-weather "advisories" to alert travelers or people who must be outdoors to weather situations that may cause inconvenience or difficulty.

Watches and Warnings

"Watches" and "warnings" are more serious than "advisories."

Watches are intended to provide enough lead time so that those who need to adjust their plans can do so. They are usually issued 24 to 48 hours in advance of the event(s). Watches generally precede warnings.

Warnings are intended to warn the public of situations that may make travel impossible or could pose a threat to life and property. Warnings are usually issued for a period of up to 12 hours in duration, but can be extended.

Forecast Tip! Some areas of the United States that usually do not get much snow in the wintertime will issue warnings at lower thresholds, like 4 inches in 12 hours, or 6 inches in 24 hours.

Forecast Tip! Sometimes the actual weather will fall short of what an advisory or warning has projected. However, if the forecaster waits until the last minute to say "The dam might break," then the public will not have time to prepare.

Regional Weather Problems

6

Avalanches, flash floods, tornadoes, and hurricanes are some of nature's most powerful forces. Each year they account for many millions of dollars in damage and the loss of life. The problems encountered by outdoor users will vary depending upon the region of the country and the time of the year.

Avalanches

In mountainous regions of North America, it is possible to encounter winterlike weather almost any time of the year. Significant snowfall can be hazardous to outdoor users who are not equipped for winter conditions.

One dangerous effect of accumulating snowfall on mountain slopes is the formation of avalanches. Even small avalanches can bury a person under enough snow that self-rescue is impossible. Forecasting when and where avalanches will occur is quite complex, and requires training and experience. The outdoor enthusiast would be wise to take a professional avalanche course before venturing into the mountains. (See *Avalanche Aware* by John Moynier [Falcon, 1998] for more information.)

The majority of avalanches occur in the winter season; however, many large and dangerous avalanches release in late spring or early summer.

In some regions of western North America, avalanche forecast centers issue daily avalanche hazard forecasts (winter season only), available by phoning an "avalanche hotline." These forecasts outline the general hazard level, ranging from low to extreme, and will give a weather forecast for the mountains. Call your local Forest or Park Service office to find out if a hotline is available in your area, or visit www.avalanche.org for avalanche forecasts on the web.

Avalanche Safety:

- Changes in precipitation, wind, and temperature affect the extent of hazard from avalanches.

- The terrain and underlying snowpack contribute to avalanche hazard.

- Most victims trigger the avalanche that kills them.

- Be able to make your own avalanche-hazard evaluation in the field.

- Check local conditions and call an avalanche hotline (if available).

- Practice avalanche search-and-rescue techniques before you go.

Flash Floods

When heavy rain falls on small stream basins, flash floods can occur. This is possible in many parts of North America, but in the Desert Southwest, flash floods can be especially hazardous to hikers venturing into narrow washes or deep canyons.

What is known as the "North American" or "Arizona Monsoon" is responsible for producing the majority of the thunderstorms—and the annual precipitation—over the southwestern United States. A "monsoon" is a seasonal wind-flow pattern. During the monsoon, warm, moist, tropical air from both the Pacific Ocean and the Gulf of Mexico moves northward over the hot, dry desert. This creates a very unstable air mass that frequently produces large thunderstorms that can turn a dry canyon into a rushing torrent in a matter of seconds.

Thunderstorms with flash-flood-producing rains are most likely to occur from late summer to early fall, or July through September.

The National Weather Service will issue flash-flood watches and warnings for areas that have the potential for strong thunderstorms producing heavy rains. Be aware of flash-flood potential anytime thunderstorms are forecast or imminent.

Flash-Flood Safety:

- Do not hike into a canyon or wash when it is raining, or if flash-flood watches have been issued.

- Consider canceling a hike if the forecast calls for *any* chance of thunderstorms.

- Be wary of any distant thunder, as the runoff from a thunderstorm miles away may be headed toward your location.

- Streams that are rising indicate rain nearby. Seek higher ground.

- If any rain begins, proceed in the fastest way possible out of a canyon and seek higher ground.

- Do not camp near streams or in washes.

Tornadoes

Tornadoes are among the most powerful, violent, and destructive weather phenomena on Earth. Seventy-five percent of the world's tornadoes occur in the United States. The majority of those occur in the Midwest, although every state, including Alaska, has seen tornadoes. Tornadoes generally form over flat ground in wide-open spaces when the atmosphere is extremely unstable. Some tornadoes have also been reported in more mountainous areas during times of strong thunderstorm activity.

Wind speeds in a violent tornado will reach 200 to 300 mph. These winds are strong enough to tear a house from its foundation, turn a car into a flying missile, or suck the asphalt off a highway. Tornadoes affect a relatively small area for a short amount of time.

Spring through early fall is the main tornado season in the United States, but tornadoes have occurred in every month of the year.

The National Weather Service issues tornado watches and warnings for specific areas. Watches may come hours ahead of time; warnings may happen only minutes ahead of the event.

Tornado Safety:

- Assuming you do not have any other shelter or a basement to hide in, lie down in a ditch or low spot.

- Protect yourself from flying debris and watch out for falling trees.

- If a large thunderstorm is moving toward you, start looking for a hiding place.

- Large hail with a thunderstorm may indicate tornado potential.

- Bulbous cloud bases forming under a cumulonimbus cloud (see chapter 7 for basic cloud types) may also indicate tornado potential.

- Waterspouts are tornadoes that touch down over water. If you are on (or in) the water, get to shore.

Hurricanes

Hurricanes are storms that form over warm ocean waters of 80 degrees F or warmer and have a sustained wind speed of greater than 74 mph. The usual progression is from a tropical depression (38 mph winds or less) to a tropical storm (39 mph to 73 mph winds) to a hurricane (winds of 74 mph and above). These storms form in the Atlantic, Caribbean, and Gulf of Mexico, as well as the eastern Pacific.

The most commonly affected parts of the country are the Gulf Coast, the southeastern United States, and the Atlantic Seaboard. Heavy rains and high winds from hurricanes can extend several hundred miles inland. Pacific hurricanes commonly move inland over Baja California and Mexico. They can send significant moisture farther north over the southwestern United States, adding moisture to the annual monsoon. Periodically, Pacific hurricanes will make landfall in Hawaii.

Damaging winds and flooding due to heavy rains are the most serious problems caused by hurricanes. Hurricanes can affect a very large area for many hours, or even days.

In the Atlantic, Caribbean, and Gulf of Mexico, the hurricane season is considered to be from June 1 to November

30. In the eastern Pacific, the season is from about May 15 to November 30.

Hurricanes are usually well advertised before making landfall. The National Weather Service's Hurricane Center issues tropical storm and hurricane watches or warnings, 24 to 36 hours ahead of time. (For flash-flood, tornado, or hurricane watches and warnings on the web, visit www.spc.noaa.gov/products/wwa.)

Hurricane Safety Tips:

- Evacuate areas that are under a hurricane watch or warning. (If unable to evacuate, be prepared for flash-flooding, and move to higher ground.)

- Hurricanes may spawn tornadoes or severe thunderstorms.

- The eye of a hurricane has the least rainfall and the calmest winds.

- The right front quarter of a hurricane contains the strongest winds.

A Word about El Niño and La Niña

El Niño and La Niña are not storms, although they can be responsible for causing a variety of unusual weather patterns across the United States. Collectively known as the El Niño / Southern Oscillation (ENSO), this is a phenomenon that is occurring in the Equatorial Pacific, which can affect weather patterns around the globe.

The ENSO actually has three different phases or events: El Niño, La Niña, and Neutral. Sea-surface temperatures between the coast of Ecuador and Indonesia determine the current state of the ENSO.

An El Niño event is occurring when sea-surface temperatures across the Equatorial Pacific are warmer than normal. La Niña is occurring when temperatures are colder than normal. Neutral ENSO conditions (No Niño) occur when temperatures are near normal, usually when transitioning between the El and La phases.

ENSO events can disrupt "normal" weather patterns around the globe, and are more notable during the Northern Hemisphere winter.

In general, during an El Niño winter, the northern tier of the United States experiences warmer than normal temperatures and below-normal precipitation, while the southern tier of the United States is usually cooler, with above-normal precipitation.

During a La Niña winter the opposite is true: The northern tier of the United States usually experiences a cooler and snowier winter, while the southern tier is usually warmer and drier.

An ENSO event changes the longer-term or seasonal weather patterns, but it should not change the way you read the day-to-day weather. A storm is still a storm. The signs, warnings, and problems associated with severe weather, at any time of the year, will remain the same.

Cloud
Watching

7

Cloud movement is our visual clue as to which way the winds aloft are blowing, and it shows the direction from which any potential weather will be coming. Cloud form identifies how stable or unstable the atmosphere is, and gives us a clue as to how far off a storm might be.

The Most Basic Cloud Forms
Clouds come in two basic forms:

1. **Stratus** clouds are flat and shallow, and indicate that the air is more stable.

2. **Cumulus** clouds are puffy and tall, and indicate that the air is unstable.

Beyond the two basic forms, the atmosphere is capable of producing a myriad of possible cloud formations. Luckily, most clouds have a common "type" and are easy to recognize. From there, the task is to puzzle out their meaning.

Cloud Types and Identification

High-Level Clouds
Clouds at altitudes between 16,500 and 40,000 feet.

CIRRUS
Description: High, thin, and wispy. Often referred to as "mare's tails" (resembles the hair on the tail of a horse).

Indication: Indicates warm air aloft. Atmosphere is stable. Usually seen several hundred miles ahead of a warm front.

CIRROSTRATUS
Description: Thin overcast layer of thicker cirrus. May see a halo around the sun or moon.

Indication: Indicates increasing moisture aloft. Normally next in line behind cirrus and ahead of a warm front.

CIRROCUMULUS
Description: A little puffier than cirrostratus. No dark bases. Often called a "mackerel sky" (resembles the pattern on a mackerel's back).

Indication: Indicates increasing moisture and some instability aloft. Too high to be a problem just yet.

Middle-Level Clouds
Clouds at altitudes between 6,500 and 16,500 feet.

ALTOSTRATUS
Description: Gray skies. The sun produces no shadows at the surface.

Indication: Impending precipitation if lowered to near-mountaintop level. (Still in stable air ahead of a warm front.)

ALTOCUMULUS
Description: Thicker, a little darker, and more globular than cirrocumulus.

Indication: These may produce showers over higher mountains. Atmosphere is becoming more unstable.

LENTICULAR

Description: These are lentil-shaped clouds that usually "cap" a mountain and resemble flying saucers.

Indication: Very high winds aloft. Moisture at a lower level than cirrostratus. Atmosphere stable.

Low-Level Clouds

Clouds with bases below 6,500 feet (can be several thousand feet thick).

STRATOCUMULUS

Description: Darker and lower than altostratus or altocumulus.

Indication: Precipitation may occur if clouds are low or thick enough.

STRATUS

Description: Low cloud cover. The thicker the layer, the darker the base.

Indication: Precipitation may be imminent. Found near warm front.

NIMBOSTRATUS

Description: Very dark and gray (nimbo is Latin for "shower").

Indication: This is a stratus cloud that produces rain or snow.

Figure 10: Clouds

All-Level Clouds
Clouds can have bases below 6,000 feet and tops above 40,000 feet.

Cumulus
Description: Usually white and puffy; can grow quite tall.

Indication: May develop into a shower or thundershower. May form in a line along a cold front. Atmosphere is unstable.

Cumulonimbus
Description: Dark bases and tall columns that may end in an anvil-shaped top.

Indication: These produce full-fledged thunderstorms. Atmosphere is very unstable. Look out!

Observe by Watching
Only the most seasoned old-timer can look up at the sky and say with impunity, "Yep, it's gonna rain tomorrow." The reason old-timers can do this is that they have seen the same progression of clouds before, and they recognize a pattern. This comes with a lot of practice and experience.

When trying to forecast weather by watching the clouds, you first have to train yourself to look at the sky more often. Observe as much of the sky as you possibly can; don't look in just in one direction.

Reading clouds is like reading palms; there may be several different interpretations of what's to come. Most importantly, when you "read" the sky, note the trends that are occurring over time. This will become one of your most valuable field forecasting tools.

Observing Cumulus Clouds

- Where no cumulus clouds appear, the air is stable or sinking.

- The more cumulus coverage there is, the more widespread the instability in the atmosphere.

- The "scattered sheep" or "fair-weather" cumulus-type clouds never develop vertically very much. Their bases stay white all day rather than turning gray, and they do not pose a threat.

- Stratocumulus clouds may spread out more than regular cumulus clouds, and they cover more of the sky, but they do not develop vertically very well because there is a stable layer of air above them.

- The faster cumulus clouds build, the more likely it is that they will turn into cumulonimbus clouds and produce thunderstorms.

Forecast Tip! Cumulus clouds generally develop more quickly and may be related to a faster-moving cold front. Cold fronts move faster than warm fronts.

Forecast Tip! Cumulus clouds indicate the atmosphere is unstable near the clouds.

Observing Stratus Clouds

- Stratus clouds indicate that the atmosphere is stable—or relatively stable—within that cloud layer.

- Stratus clouds indicate that warmer air is above cooler air.

- Stratus clouds generally develop slowly and are usually related to a warm front. Warm fronts move more slowly than cold fronts.

- High cirrus or cirrostratus clouds are usually related to a warm front that is still hundreds of miles away from your location.

Forecast Tip! Cirrus or cirrostratus clouds may mean that precipitation will come within 24 to 48 hours.

Forecast Tip! The progression of clouds from cirrus to altostratus is a good indication that precipitation may be coming within 12 to 36 hours.

Forecast Tip! A progression from altostratus down to a lowering stratus cloud layer is the best indication that precipitation is coming within 12 hours.

Cloud Watchers Checklist

❑ Check height and bases to determine the elevation or altitude of the clouds. Is the trend toward lowering or rising bases? Do the clouds look as if they are threatening to produce rain or snow?

❑ Check type to determine if the clouds might be associated with a warm front or a cold front. Is the atmosphere stable or unstable?

❏ Check direction to determine if the clouds are coming from a direction consistent with an approaching storm. (This will vary from region to region in the United States.)

❏ Check coverage to determine if the clouds are becoming more or less organized. Is the trend toward increasing or decreasing cloud cover?

❏ Check thickness to determine how much moisture the cloud contains. If the cloud is right over you, a darker base indicates a thicker cloud with more moisture.

> *Forecast Tip!* A mix of cloud types in the sky at the same time paints a more chaotic and uncertain weather picture.

Fog

Fog is a stratus cloud, the base of which is near ground level. It forms when air near the surface cools and water vapor in the air condenses. There are three main types of fog, which form for different reasons:

1. **Valley fog** forms when the air cools to the dew point. If there is only moisture right at the ground, then only dew (or frost) will form. If there is also some moisture in the lower levels of the atmosphere—for example, from recent precipitation—then fog and dew (or frost) can form.

Valley fog usually forms overnight during times of high pressure, clear skies, a stable atmosphere, and calm winds. Once the sun rises and warms the air so that it is several degrees above the dew point, the fog burns off. A thick fog in the valley usually means clear skies above in the mountains.

2. **Sea fog** forms when a layer of warmer air moves horizontally over cold ground or water. Sea fog forms in coastal areas when warmer, tropical air moves over the relatively colder ocean water. In the central and eastern United States, sea fog forms when moist air from the Gulf of Mexico moves northward over colder ground. In addition, sea fogs are often carried inland along the West Coast of the United States and Canada.

3. **Mountain fog** forms when humid air at low levels is blown up a mountain by the wind. This commonly occurs in the plains along the east slope of the Rockies. By the same process, clouds will hang along a hill or mountainside, especially after recent rain or snow.

The Red Sky Proverb

Red sky at night, sailor's delight. Red in morning, sailor take warning.

On many clear mornings or evenings, you can look toward the rising or setting sun and see a red sky. This is usually due to dust or smog trapped in the lower levels of the atmosphere. For this old adage to be valid, you do not look toward the sunrise or sunset; you look away from it, toward the opposite horizon.

How to Use the Red Sky Proverb Properly:

In the morning: If the bases of the clouds are red to the west at sunrise, bad weather may be coming within the next 12 to 24 hours.

In the evening: If the bases of the clouds are red to the east at sunset, bad weather is leaving, and good weather should be coming for the next 12 to 24 hours.

> *Forecast Tip!* This red sky proverb will only be useful in the midlatitudes of the United States, where the prevailing winds blow from west to east. Remember, it is the redness of the clouds you are looking for, not a red haze in the air.

Weather Tools

8

Once you step outside, you are leaving behind that portion of weather knowledge available from television and the Internet. If you are taking an extended trip into the outdoors (for example, a weeklong backpacking trip), then the forecast information you have when you leave will quickly expire. Fortunately, there are some other tools you can take with you to rely on for weather guidance.

Eyeballs and Brain

Become weather-wise by looking, listening, and feeling for changes in the weather. Use your knowledge of clouds and their meanings as one observational tool, but also use your senses to give you clues about how the atmosphere is changing. Ask yourself why the air feels the way it does, and how it has changed.

Wind speed or direction changes, even subtle ones, are often your first indication that the weather is changing. Increasing winds may indicate a front approaching or a strong pressure gradient nearby. If clouds aloft are moving at a high rate of speed, then perhaps the jet stream is bringing a storm system your way.

Temperature changes from day to day are an indication that the air mass has changed or that a front has passed. You do not necessarily need a thermometer to read these changes; you can sense if temperatures are becoming warmer or colder. Try to relate that information to which way the wind is blowing and how it may have changed.

Humidity is relatively easy to detect. You can sense when the air feels damp, like on a foggy morning or a muggy summer afternoon. You can almost smell the water vapor in the air, and most people would agree that rain has a distinct smell. Dry air is also recognizable because it creates more dust in the air and irritates our nasal passages.

Pressure in the atmosphere can change quickly while the pressure inside your body does not change quite as fast. Thus, there can be a pressure gradient between you and the atmosphere. When your knee aches, it may be because you have relatively high pressure inside your joint, while the air pressure outside is getting lower. Sensing these changes is using your body as a barometer.

Barometers and Altimeters

Many types of barometers are available, from simple wall-hanging types to wristwatch models with barometer and altimeter functions. More-expensive models are usually more accurate. If the pressure in the atmosphere is changing, then you can expect a change in the weather. How drastically the weather changes will depend on how much and how fast the pressure is changing. These changes in pressure can be monitored with either a barometer or an altimeter, both of which measure changes in air pressure.

Barometers give you a reading of air pressure. The most commonly used scales to measure air pressure are inches of mercury (in. Hg) or millibars (mb).

Altimeters give you a reading of altitude (elevation above sea level) and act essentially as barometers. Altimeters measure in feet or meters.

As you gain altitude, you have less atmosphere above you, so a barometer will read a lower pressure while an altimeter records a higher elevation.

- Barometers fall (altimeters gain elevation) as air pressure decreases.

- Barometers rise (altimeters lose elevation) as air pressure increases.

> **Forecast Tip!** A change of 1,000 feet of elevation equates to about 1 inch of mercury. So, 100 feet equals 0.10 in. Hg, while 10 feet equals 0.01 in. Hg.

Monitoring Barometric Pressure

The best time to monitor your barometer or altimeter is when you are stationary (for example, at home or in camp). The amount and direction of change over time is more important than the actual reading.

- If the barometer is falling (altimeter gains elevation) at the rates in Table 16, then expect the weather to worsen.

- If the barometer is rising (altimeter loses elevation) at the rates in Table 16, then expect the weather to improve.

There will be some daily fluctuation in the barometer even when the weather is not changing. Expect an increase of about 0.04 in. Hg (1 mb) at about 10 a.m. and again at about 10 p.m. Expect a decrease of about the same amount by roughly 4 a.m. and 4 p.m. In Alaska these changes are near zero, while near the equator changes can more than double.

Forecast Tip! Barometric pressure changes are a less-reliable indicator of weather changes near the equator or in northern latitudes around 60 degrees north. This is primarily due to the large area of semipermanent low pressure that resides at both of these latitudes.

Forecast Tip! When climbing mountains above approximately 10,000 feet, pressure decreases with height less rapidly, so changes on the barometer will be more subtle. This issue warrants further study, but when you are climbing mountains at higher altitudes, you can expect smaller changes on the barometer to mean bigger or more-rapid weather changes than the Barometer/Altimeter Forecaster indicates (see Table 16).

Table 16: Barometer/Altimeter Forecaster			
Barometer Change in. Hg (mb)	Altimeter Change feet (meters)	Time (hours)	Weather Change Expected
.04 to .07 (1 to 2)	40 to 70 (12 to 20)	3	Some changes should be expected. May be slow to develop.
.08 + (2.5 +)	80 + (24 +)	3	Significant changes should be expected. May be developing rapidly.
.20 to .40 (6 to 12)	200 to 400 (60 to 120)	12 to 24	Some changes should be expected. May be slow to develop.
.40 + (12 +)	400 + (120 +)	12 to 24	Significant changes should be expected. May be developing rapidly.

Wind Speed

An easy way to estimate wind speed is to observe how trees move or how waves form on a lake. Estimates will vary somewhat depending on the species and stoutness of the tree, or on the size, depth, and temperature of the lake. However, this "visual wind-speed gauge" should be close enough for most purposes (see Table 17).

Table 17: Visual Wind Speed Gauge	
Speed (mph)	What You Observe on Land or Lake
Calm	Smoke rises straight up. Fog can form. Water is glassy.
5 to 10	Smoke drifts. Leaves rustle. Ripples or small waves form.
10 to 20	Dust moves. Twigs and small branches move. Whitecaps start to form.
20 to 30	Small trees and large branches move. Lots of whitecaps: large waves form.
30 to 40	Small branches break, big trees sway. Walking is harder. Waves break.
40 to 50	Small or dead trees blow down. Must lean into wind to walk. High waves.
50 to 60	"Gale Force" winds. Large trees snap. Walking very difficult. Very high waves.
60 to 70	"Storm Force" winds. Difficult to stand. Waves very, very high.
74 +	"Hurricane Force." Batten down the hatches!

Forecast Tip! The force of the wind increases exponentially as the speed increases; for example, a 40 mph wind is not twice as strong as a 20 mph wind—it is four times as strong.

Radio or Weather Radio

Most AM and FM radio stations will broadcast the local weather forecast at least once an hour, and announce any severe weather watches or warnings more frequently. Reception of am radio stations will be best at night (just be sure you are not listening to a station from Los Angeles while backpacking in Colorado).

National Oceanic and Atmospheric Administration (NOAA) Weather Radio operates on seven different VHF frequencies between 162.425 and 162.550 MHz, and broadcasts from the nearest National Weather Service office. It is available in most locations across all fifty states, 24 hours a day, seven days a week. Canada also has a similar weather radio system.

Most weather radios available from electronics suppliers have all seven frequencies programmed in. Simply tune to the one that has the strongest signal. NOAA Weather Radio also streams their broadcasts on the Internet for many locations.

The continuous recording on the weather radio includes current weather observations, a discussion of current weather patterns, local zone forecast information, extended outlooks, and more. Some weather radios also come equipped with an alarm system that can be set to go off automatically when a severe weather watch or warning is issued from the local National Weather Service office.

The weather radio is an incredibly useful tool for any extended trip. Mountains may block some transmissions, but for an update, try tuning in when you are on a ridgetop.

Field Forecasting

9

When forecasting weather from the field, do not expect to be able to make predictions very far into the future. Most of the time, a fairly accurate 12- to 24-hour forecast is a reasonable aim. Utilize all of the tools and information available, and be systematic when gathering information. Constantly be looking for changes or trends, even when the weather is good.

The Input: Organize and Analyze the Information

Knowledge of Local Weather
The more "weather-dependent" the outing (that is, one that could be delayed or canceled or become hazardous due to bad weather), the more you need to know about the local weather. If you are completely unfamiliar with the location where you are going, then do a little climate research first.

Local climate information will provide you with a good general picture of what the weather should be like at certain times of the year. Find out what the normal high and low temperatures are, what the average monthly precipitation is, and, if possible, the extremes that have been recorded for these variables.

Climate information is readily available for major cities and some smaller towns. For more-remote locations, try calling the nearest chamber of commerce or a local fishing shop or mountaineering store. Ask them, "What is it normally like there this time of year, and is this a good time to come and do this activity?"

Call the closest National Weather Service office to find out which direction bad weather usually comes from. This will vary for different geographic locations in the United States. Ask them, "What weather patterns commonly bring bad weather to the area, and what is the most serious weather problem that might be experienced there at this time of year?"

Knowledge of Local Terrain

It is also important to know if the local terrain is going to influence the weather. Climate information and forecasts for a valley location, for example, may not hold true at higher elevations in the nearby mountains. Temperature, wind, and precipitation amount can change dramatically with a small gain in elevation. To identify elevation changes in the area you will be visiting, refer to topographic maps from the US Geological Survey, and ask at the local National Weather Service office how local topography may affect the weather.

Latest Weather Forecast

Weather is like a soap opera: You have to watch it every day to keep up with what is going on. At home, stay updated by listening to the forecasts and noting their accuracy. Before departing on a trip, pay attention to current and forecasted conditions in your destination area. Once in the field, get updates from the weather radio if possible.

Yesterday's Weather

Backcasting is easier than forecasting. Reviewing the previous day's weather may hold some clues about tomorrow's weather. Take into account changes that you observed over the past 24 hours. What were the clouds doing? What did the barometer do? Relate that information to what was said in the forecast.

Did your observations match the previous day's forecasted weather?

- If yes, then have some confidence that subsequent forecasts will also be accurate.

- If no, then ask yourself why not, and look for other clues to explain why the weather was different from the forecast. Is local terrain playing a part? Do you need to know more about local weather patterns? Or perhaps the weather is changing too rapidly for an accurate forecast; if so, you may need to discount what the previous day's forecast said and move forward with your observations as your best baseline information.

Today's Weather

Run through the same drill as you did in assessing yesterday's weather: Observe the clouds and note any changes in barometric pressure or wind direction and speed over the last 12 to 24 hours, paying particular attention to trends.

Are the observations you are making right now matching the forecasted weather for today?

- If yes, then the timing of the weather corresponds well with the forecast, and your confidence should be high.

- If no, then try to explain why not, with the observations you are making. Is local terrain influencing the weather? Could the forecasted weather be missing your location? Or, is the forecast timing off; that is, is it starting earlier than forecast, or has it not yet started?

Build a Forecast Pyramid

Organize all of the information you have gathered into a field forecast pyramid. Every day, reevaluate each block of the pyramid and try to answer the question in the top block.

Figure 11: Forecast pyramid

The Output: Make a Forecast

Ultimately, your field forecast is trying to answer one of the following questions:

1. If the weather is good now, when will it worsen, and what are the signs?

2. If the weather is bad now, when will it improve, and what are the signs?

To get an answer, you must consider all of the information you have gathered and analyzed. You can make a forecast with less information, but your confidence may not be as high if some of the input is missing or unavailable.

> **Forecast Tip!** Without any input, you are reduced to doing an "OTW" (Out the Window) forecast. Use caution with this method, because OTW forecasts tend to have a very short shelf life.

Signs of Worsening Weather

1. **Falling barometer.** A rapidly falling barometer (altimeter gaining elevation), even without the presence of increasing clouds, is an indication that something is changing on the horizon. You just can't see it yet. A steadily falling barometer, coupled with increasing high clouds that continue to lower and thicken with time, usually foretells an approaching storm system. A halo around the sun or moon means high clouds and moisture are starting to increase. If clouds continue to lower and thicken over the next 6 to 12 hours, and the barometer is falling slowly, then expect

some precipitation within the next 12 to 24 hours. Generally, the progression from halo to rain (or snow) takes about 18 to 36 hours.

2. **Warming with falling barometer.** Warming temperatures and a steadily falling barometer, along with winds blowing from a southerly direction, often precede a storm system.

3. **Rapidly building cumulus clouds.** Cumulus clouds (summer season) that build rapidly as the day starts to warm usually lead to afternoon thunderstorms.

4. **Lenticular clouds and lowering clouds.** Lenticular clouds over mountains, when followed within the next 12 hours by lowering and thickening clouds, usually mean a warm front is approaching. You may see precipitation at lower elevations 24 hours or so after lenticulars form—sooner over the mountains—or you may experience it immediately if you are up near the clouds themselves.

Signs of Improving Weather

1. **Heavier precipitation during a storm.** The heaviest precipitation during a storm or thunderstorm often comes near the end of the storm. This may be your earliest sign that the weather will be improving over the next 3 to 12 hours.

2. **Cooling and rising barometer.** Cooling temperatures and a rapidly rising barometer, along with a wind shift to a more-northerly direction, usually signal that a cold front has passed.

3. **Rising barometer and clearing.** A steadily rising barometer coupled with decreasing clouds is almost a sure bet that weather is improving.

4. **Cloud breaks.** Breaks in clouds (especially in lower clouds), with no higher clouds visible above the breaks, may indicate that a storm is almost over.

5. **Cloud bases rising.** Cloud bases rising and precipitation decreasing may mean a warm front has passed. A barometer rising steadily for 12 hours or more signals high pressure is on the way.

Signs of Something between Good and Bad

1. **Lenticulars without thicker clouds.** When lenticular clouds are not followed by any other lower or thicker clouds, this may simply indicate high winds aloft, and possibly a jet stream nearby. Pressure stops rising, then starts to fall.

2. **Showers mixed with sun breaks.** When showers are interspersed with good weather, the barometer does not fluctuate much, and winds are variable, there may be persistent instability or a series of smaller upper-level disturbances cycling through.

3. **Multiple precipitation types.** A mix of precipitation types may signal an occluded front nearby. The barometer may not move much, or it may fluctuate up and down. If the associated storm system keeps moving, the weather will improve; if it stalls, it will not.

Signs of Continued Good Weather

1. **No clouds and steadily rising barometer.**

2. **Barometer is high and steady.**

3. **Cirrus clouds.** Fair-weather cirrus clouds (high, thin, wispy, and scattered) drifting by, generally coming from a northwesterly direction. This indicates that you are in the early, or front, part of a high-pressure ridge.

4. **Dew or frost with no fog in the mornings.**

5. **Fog in the morning that burns off quickly.**

6. **No afternoon clouds.** No afternoon buildup of cumulus clouds (summer season) indicates a very dry and stable atmosphere.

> *Forecast Tip!* When the pressure is high during good weather, note the barometric pressure. It will probably have to rise back to that point after a storm passes in order for the weather to be good again.
>
> *Forecast Tip!* If the forecast you heard says "sunny" and you are getting rain or snow, trust your observations and make your own forecast.
>
> *Forecast Tip!* A "persistence" forecast will be correct about 50 percent of the time; that is, "tomorrow's weather will be like today's."

Forecast Tip! "Backing" winds change in a counterclockwise direction (for example, from NW to SW). Backing winds usually indicate that bad weather and low pressure are approaching.

Forecast Tip! "Veering" winds change in a clockwise direction (for example, from SW to NW). Veering winds usually indicate that good weather and high pressure are approaching. To keep this straight, remember, "veering means clearing."

Decision Making: "Go" or "No Go" Forecasting

10

Once you have formulated a forecast, the only remaining question to ask is: Will it be possible to complete your activity based on the current and forecasted weather? In order to make that decision, you have to evaluate three factors that are indirectly related to the weather: the activity, your ability, and the risk involved.

Evaluate the Activity

Type of Activity: Is this a picnic, hike, bike ride, golf game, paragliding flight, rock climb, ski tour, or a major expedition? Do you consider this activity to be hazardous?

Location of Activity: Are you going around the block, into the mountains, or to a strange and remote corner of the Earth?

Duration of Activity: Will this take an hour, a day, a week, or a month? Do you have enough time to complete this activity?

Evaluate Your Ability

Experience Level: Do you consider yourself (and the rest of your group) to be skilled at this activity?

Knowledge Level: How familiar are you with the area and its weather conditions?

Preparation Level: How well equipped are you for this activity, and for the weather?

Evaluate the Risk

What is your "risk tolerance"? Is it high or low?

Subjective Risk Level: If you get injured during this activity, can you take care of yourself, and how difficult would an evacuation be?

Objective Risk Level: If the weather gets bad, can you easily retreat to shelter?

Survivability Level: If you had to stay out in bad weather, how long could you survive?

Guidelines for "Go" or "No Go" Forecasting

Timing is everything in forecasting. Even on their best day, top meteorologists have a hard time being exact with the timing of weather systems. Don't feel bad if your timing is off. There is no way to be 100 percent accurate with the weather, especially when it is in a near-constant state of change.

Timing is everything in high-risk outdoor sports as well. You have to realize that the weather may not be ideal right now to do what you want to do. Maybe it would be wise to wait for a better day.

- Don't let your goals cloud your thinking or change your forecast.

- If there is uncertainty in the forecast, then there should be some uncertainty in your plans.

- Forecasting is an ongoing process. Constantly reevaluate whether or not you should proceed.

- Imagine the worst weather scenario for the day. What would be the consequences of being caught out in that weather?

- Predicting the weather will always be an inexact science, so leave yourself a wide margin of safety.

- Exercise common sense.

Overestimating your ability and underestimating the weather is a bad combination.

The Decision

First, decide if you want to do this activity, given the current and forecasted weather.

If the answer is no, then stay home.

If yes, then proceed to the "Go" or "No Go" Scoresheet (see Table 18).

Options:

1. **Go:** Keep going, and count on the weather not getting worse.

2. **No Go:** Turn around now, and be safe.

3. **Stall:** Wait and see if the weather gets better or worse.

"Go" or "No Go" Scenario

The Plan: It is midsummer and you are going for a weekend climb of Mount Fictitious in the Rocky Mountains with two friends. Mount Fictitious's summit elevation is 14,000 feet. The plan is to leave early Saturday and make the 3-hour drive to the trailhead, at the 7,000-foot elevation. From there, it will take most of the day to hike the 8 miles to your base camp at 11,000 feet. The climb on Sunday is expected to be about a 9-hour round-trip from base camp; then it will take another 4 hours or so to hike back to the trailhead Sunday evening.

Table 18: "Go" or "No Go" Scoresheet				
Evaluate Activity	0	1	2	Score
Hazardous?	Yes	Sort of	No	
Location	Remote	Sort of	Not Remote	
Duration	Long	Sort of	Short	
Evaluate Ability	0	1	2	
Experience	Not Skilled	Sort of	Very Skilled	
Knowledge	Unfamiliar	Sort of	Very Familiar	
Preparation	Poorly Equipped	Sort of	Well Equipped	
Evaluate Risk	0	1	2	
Self Rescue Possible?	No	Maybe	Yes	
Retreat Possible?	No	Maybe	Yes	
Survive Overnight?	No	Maybe	Yes	
Evaluate Weather	0	1	2	
What is Your Forecast?	Getting Worse	Staying the Same	Getting Better	
			Total Score:	
• Consider a "Go" if total score is comfortably above 10.				
• Consider a "No Go" if total score is 10 or below.				

Everyone in the party considers this climb to be "sort of" hazardous. Two of you are experienced climbers; the third member of your party is less experienced. You are all "sort of" familiar with the area and the weather, but no one in your party has climbed this mountain before. Everyone is well equipped for the climb and for the weather. There is some first-aid experience among the group, but minimal rescue knowledge. The upper half of the mountain is notoriously difficult to retreat from, especially in bad weather. Nobody is prepared to spend a night out, but all could probably survive one.

The Weather: On Saturday morning you rise early to check the weather before making the 3-hour drive to the trailhead. You check:

1. current and forecast weather maps;

2. latest "synopsis" or weather discussion;

3. local and extended forecast; and

4. satellite and radar.

- The current weather map shows high pressure over your destination, a low-pressure center off the Pacific Northwest coast, and a cold front near the coast. The forecast map shows the cold front still west of Mount Fictitious on Sunday afternoon, and the jet stream closer to the area.

- Satellite and radar loops at 6 a.m. showed clouds and showers moving across the Pacific Northwest.

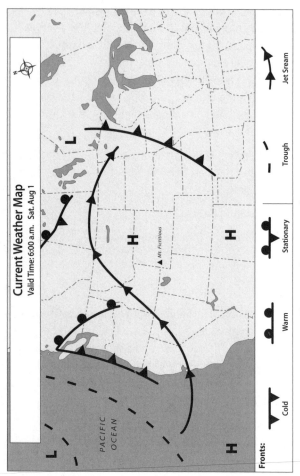

Figure 12: Current weather map

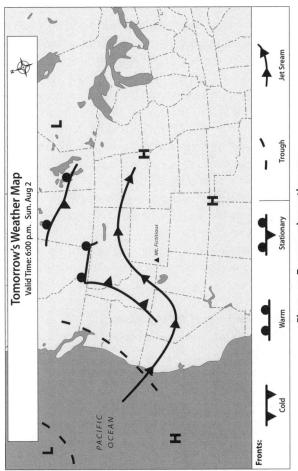

Figure 13: Tomorrow's weather map

The Synopsis:

STATE FORECAST DISCUSSION ISSUED 3 A.M. MDT, SATURDAY, AUGUST 1.

A RIDGE OF HIGH PRESSURE THAT HAS BEEN OVER THE STATE THE LAST SEVERAL DAYS WILL BEGIN TO FLATTEN AND SHIFT EAST FOR THE NEXT COUPLE OF DAYS. DEVELOPING LOW-PRESSURE SYSTEM MOVING SOUTH FROM THE GULF OF ALASKA AND ASSOCIATED COLD FRONT WILL MOVE ACROSS THE PACIFIC NORTHWEST IN THE NEXT 24 HOURS. COMPUTER MODELS ARE CONSISTENT WITH MOVING COLD FRONT ACROSS WESTERN PORTIONS OF THE STATE BY EARLY MONDAY ALONG WITH STRONG WSW JET. THE BEST CONVECTION AND MOST UNSTABLE AIR WILL BE FOCUSED ALONG OR AHEAD OF COLD FRONT WITH POTENTIAL FOR ISOLATED STRONG THUNDERSTORMS TO DEVELOP IN THE WESTERN HALF OF THE STATE SUNDAY NIGHT AND DURING THE DAY MONDAY IN THE EAST HALF OF THE STATE. UPPER TROF BEHIND SYSTEM TO MOVE ACROSS THE STATE LATER MONDAY COOLING TEMPS AND MAY KEEP SHOWERS AROUND MOST OF THE STATE INTO TUESDAY.

Note: In all National Weather Service discussions, the text may be heavily abbreviated and can be difficult to read. For example, "trof" is commonly used for "trough."

The Local Forecast and Extended Outlook:

FICTITIOUS VALLEY AND SURROUNDING COMMUNITIES, 5 A.M. MDT, SATURDAY, AUGUST 1.

TODAY . . . MOSTLY SUNNY WITH A 30 PERCENT CHANCE OF AFTERNOON OR EVENING THUNDERSTORMS. HIGHS NEAR 75. TONIGHT . . . MOSTLY CLEAR SKIES. LOWS AROUND 40. TOMORROW . . . PARTLY CLOUDY AND BREEZY BY AFTERNOON WITH A 50 PERCENT CHANCE OF THUNDERSTORMS. HIGH AROUND 70.

EXTENDED OUTLOOK FOR MONDAY AND TUESDAY . . . MOSTLY CLOUDY, BREEZY AND COOLER WITH A CHANCE OF SHOWERS AND THUNDERSTORMS EACH DAY. HIGHS AROUND 65.

Questions and Answers

Q: What should the temperature be during the day at 11,000 feet? At 14,000 feet? (**Hint:** Air cools at about 4 degrees F per 1,000 feet.)

A: To make the math easy, estimate that air is cooling at 5 degrees for every 1,000 feet. If the forecast high at 7,000 feet is 70 degrees, 4,000 feet higher it should be 20 degrees cooler, or a high temperature of 50 degrees. At 14,000 feet (7,000 feet above the valley floor), the temperature during the day might be more like 35 degrees.

Q: What would you estimate the winds to be at ridgetop level? (**Hint:** Wind speed at ridgetops is about double the valley speed.)

A: The forecast for the valley said "breezy" by afternoon. "Breezy" by definition means 15 to 25 mph winds; double that for the ridgetops, and you might expect 30 mph to 50 mph winds in the worst-case scenario.

Q: What would you expect the coldest wind-chill temperature to be on the mountain? (**Hint:** Refer to the Wind-Chill Chart on page 50.)

A: With a wind speed of 30 mph and a temperature of 30 degrees in the afternoon on the summit, you should expect the wind-chill factor to make it feel like it is around 15 degrees F.

Q: Would you expect a higher probability of thunderstorms in the mountains vs. the valley?

(**Hint:** Review thunderstorm and lightning facts on pages 41–46).

A: Thunderstorms occur more frequently over mountains than they do in valleys, so you can bet that the chances for thunderstorms at the summit are going to be better than 50/50.

The Approach: On the hike in, you notice the first cumulus clouds around 1 p.m. You first hear thunder at around 3 p.m., and you estimate it to be about 3 miles away. The first thunderstorm to produce lightning and rain showers right over you comes around 4 p.m. Judging from the cloud movement, the thunderstorms seem to have tracked from the southwest. When you arrive at base camp, there is some small hail on the ground. (You note that this seems to be better than a "30 percent chance" where you are!) Skies clear around 8:30 p.m. The wind is now from the west, coming through the pass where you are camped. You set the altimeter to the elevation of the camp, 11,000 feet, so that you can note the change when you wake up. Somebody forgot the weather radio.

The Climb: The plan was to get up by 5 a.m. and be climbing by 7 a.m., so as to be off the summit and back down to camp by 3 p.m., beating any thunderstorms. However, the alarm clock failed to do its job, and you are now 2 hours behind schedule.

The sky is still mostly clear, with what looks like a line of clouds on the western horizon. The altimeter reads 11,200 feet when you leave base camp at 9 a.m.; you reset it back to 11,000 feet. (What does that indicate?)

By noontime, you notice some cumulus clouds building off to the west. An hour later, the cumulus are building taller and are covering more of the sky, with darker-looking bases. You estimate that you are about halfway to the summit of Mount Fictitious from base camp, and if you maintain the current pace, you will arrive at the summit by 4 p.m.

What are you going to do?

A) Go up

B) Go back

C) Stall

What information are you basing your decision on?

The Decision: Based on the weather information you analyzed yesterday morning, and the fact that the altimeter indicates falling pressure, you predict that the weather will be worse tomorrow. The consequences of spending the night in a storm are potentially dangerous, especially if strong thunderstorms do materialize Sunday night. Being caught near the summit in any thunderstorm is also not desirable.

Thunderstorms are developing a little earlier than they did yesterday. No thunder has been heard yet, but yesterday's 30 percent chance of thunderstorms for the valley produced lightning, rain, and hail in the mountains. You deduce that today's "50 percent chance" will result in the same, or maybe worse, with more unstable air headed your way. At this rate, you figure that lightning, and rain or hail, may start as early as 3 p.m. Therefore, you could deduce that there is a good chance thunderstorms will begin before your party can make the summit.

You are a fairly experienced group, but you got started late and are moving more slowly than anticipated. You are unfamiliar with the mountain, and retreat is known to be difficult from this point on.

- A *prudent* party would turn around now, with a good margin of safety.

- Stalling to see what the weather does is wasting valuable time.

- A party more familiar with the climb, or with a higher *risk tolerance,* might go for it. But unless they were moving much faster—for instance, as a party of two—they would likely still encounter thunderstorms near the summit.

The preceding scenario is perhaps a more-extreme example of weather dangers encountered on a technical mountain-climbing trip. However, you can use the same commonsense approach when making weather decisions for almost any outdoor activity in almost any environment, from deserts to coastal areas.

Adapt the "Go" or "No Go" Scoresheet to fit your activity and climate, but realize that in some situations, the score can change as rapidly as the weather.

A short day hike into a narrow desert canyon, for example, would not seem like a particularly dangerous activity. A simple day hike does not require the intense preparation and fancy equipment of a climbing expedition, but you still have to be careful with the weather. With the knowledge that just a slight chance of thunderstorms even miles away can cause a life-threatening flash flood through the canyon, you need to make a similar potentially lifesaving decision to go or not go. Although day hiking in the Utah desert or exploring the California coast may never be as dangerous as climbing

Everest, weather can make any outdoor activity suddenly dangerous. Carefully planning the timing of your hike can mean the difference between avoiding Mother Nature's fury and being caught in it.

Afterword

Some Final Weather Wisdom

There is a lot of information in this book, and there is also an incredible amount of data available from other sources, but all this information is not enough. Experience is the best teacher, and this book—or the latest technology—is no substitute for that.

Accept the fact that you will be wrong about the weather, perhaps more often than you are right. Do not expect a magic formula that works every time. Hopefully, enough advice and wisdom have worked their way into these pages to enable you to read nature's warning signals.

My many years of working as a rescue ranger in the Tetons have, sadly, brought me in contact with people who paid the ultimate price at the hands of the weather.

If this book prevents just one weather-related tragedy, it will have been worth all the effort.

Appendix

Resources

Further Reading
Meteorology: The Atmosphere and the Science of Weather
by J. Moran, M. Morgan, and P. Pauley
Prentice Hall Publishers
ISBN 0-13-266701-0

The Weather Book (USA Today)
by Jack Williams
Vintage Books
ISBN 0-679-77665-6

Internet Weather Sources
AccuWeather (www.accuweather.com)
IPS MeteoStar (wxweb.meteostar.com)
MountainWeather (www.mountainweather.com)
NOAA's National Weather Service (www.nws.gov)
The Weather Channel (www.weather.com)

Index

About the Author

Jim Woodmencey grew up hiking, backpacking, and, eventually, climbing in the Sierras. In his college years he worked as a summer mountain guide in the Cascade and Alaska Ranges.

He received a bachelor of science in meteorology from Montana State University in 1982, and then spent a winter working at the Alaska Avalanche Forecast Center as an avalanche and mountain weather forecaster.

Since then, Jim has lived in Jackson, Wyoming, where he spent fourteen summers working as a climbing and rescue ranger for Grand Teton National Park, and twenty winters as a helicopter ski guide.

Jim established his own weather consulting business, MountainWeather, in 1991, and he currently works as the on-air meteorologist for the local radio station, forecasting the weather for Jackson Hole and the Teton Mountains. In his spare time he teaches both avalanche- and weather-forecasting courses. You can learn more about Jim and MountainWeather at www.mountainweather.com.

Jim is a member of the American Meteorological Society, and is certified as an instructor with the American Avalanche Association.